SECRETS OF

7 Social Emotional Learning

Tierica Berry

7 Secrets to social Emotional Learning

Published by:
Affirmative Expression
PO Box 360856
Decatur, GA 30036

Printed in the United States of America

ISBN: 978-1-7323598-5-7

FOREWORD

In every generation there arises an authentic voice to inform, inspire, and empower masses of people in need.

Couple this with the fact that most teachers and school leaders have the best of intentions but remain ill-equipped and under-prepared to deal effectively with the increasing numbers of students who have experienced emotionally crippling trauma.

Tierica Berry is that authentic voice for such a time as this, who is equipping educators and students alike.

Tierica's transparent and transformative approach has endeared her to thousands of youth across the nation and those serve them. In her own unique ways, she assists those she serves with tools and techniques to deal effectively with their own emotions. Her willingness to be her own research subject adds to her authenticity.

So adept and skillful is she, that I asked her to be the Social Emotional Learning Specialist for the Teacher Transformation Institute. I have also invited her to present to my classes in educational leadership at Clark Atlanta University. Amidst her already very demanding schedule as a national speaker, author, and consultant, she obliged and has blessed innumerable educators, leaders, and students that we serve nationally.

In order to meet the needs of today's students, her mindset and skillset is not optional, but *essential*. Every teacher, administrator, student, and parent need the skills Ms. Berry teaches and all will be much better off with them. Not only do I highly recommend her books and trainings, I have gained tremendous insight into my own emotional patterns of thought and action as a result of participating in her seminars.

This is not just a book to be read, but to be read and re-read as a rich resource and action guide. And, if you are fortunate, perhaps you will be able to have a visit to your school or school system from Tierica Berry.

Chike Akua, Ph.D., Professor and Author
Clark Atlanta University
Education for Transformation: The Keys to Releasing the Genius of African American Students

CONTENTS

ACKNOWLEDGMENTS

"No one who achieves success does so without the help of others. The wise and confident acknowledge this help with gratitude."

– Alfred North Whitehead

Thank you God for ordering my steps and showing me that I have what it takes, I am more than enough and with you anything is possible!

Dr. Akua, thank you for challenging me to share this message with the world and holding me accountable to completion.

MaRonda X, thank you for believing in my vision and walking with me every step of the way. I am honored to have you on my team and blessed to call you friend. I look forward to the blessings that are in store for us!

Last but certainly not least, Jonathan, thank you for being patient with me and supporting my mission, my vision, and me walking in my purpose.

The list of contributors to support me along my journey is long and I am grateful for each and every person. I am grateful for those who have been here since the beginning, those with whom I have parted ways, and those to recently join me on my journey.

Because of all of you I am…

INTRODUCTION

I want to start with a confession. I began this journey for selfish reasons. When I think about the great thought leaders and philanthropists of our time, I imagine them embarking on their philanthropic pursuits with the greater good in mind. I imagine them drafting plans to save humanity. However, my journey started a little differently.

Growing up as a girl of color in the suburbs of Atlanta on the more affluent side than some of my counterparts, I would say I was pretty fortunate. However, this lifestyle was not free of challenges and emotional trauma. I was a victim of bullying, sexual molestation, and sexual assault. I also struggled with self-confidence, promiscuity, and less-than-average academic success. These experiences led to a downward spiral emotionally. I never took an attempt on my life, but I remember suicidal ideations such as, "What if I weren't here?" "If I were to commit suicide, how would I do it?" "How would my family feel?" "Would it hurt?" There was a point when I would look in the mirror and just cry.

When I was younger, I was always seen as the "Happy Child," so I hid emotions from my family for fear of what the response would be. School seemed to be the place for reading, writing, and arithmetic... **_NOT_** expressing how I was feeling. There was no place for learning how to cope with emotionally traumatic experiences and when I would share these things with my friends, they would give the best advice they could, which resulted in the "blind leading the blind." I didn't know where to go or what to do with these emotions and experiences. I began writing poetry, which seemed to relieve some of my tension. Outside of my poetic expression, I picked up the risky habit of emotional suppression, which periodically resulted in unexplained crying fits or moodiness.

I was well into my twenties when I said, "enough is enough." I was tired of making mistakes, I was tired of crying, and I was tired of not knowing. Therefore, I asked myself four questions:

1. *Why am I like this?*
2. *Why am I lacking quality relationships?*
3. *What can I do to change?*
4. *To whom/what should I change?*

My research into personal development began with journaling, reading books, watching videos, attending conferences, and gathering information on mental health first aid. I became certified as an Emotional Intelligence Assessor. I learned so much throughout this process and, more importantly, I was able to find answers to my questions, make necessary changes, and was able to achieve what I call, *"Emotional Success."*

In hindsight, I realized I had inadvertently created a Social Emotional Learning (SEL) program. Those four questions were the core components of my SEL process.

Why am I like this?

(SELF AWARENESS)

Exploring this question prompted me to study myself in every way possible, including emotionally, physically, and psychologically. I learned about my strengths, weakness, likes, dislikes, and triggers.

Why am I lacking quality relationships?

(RELATIONSHIPS)

This question caused me to take a critical look at the people around me and learn about different personality types, improve my communication skills, develop interpersonal skills, and increase empathy for others. This also helped me appreciate the fact that, for better or worse, we are all guilty by association. With this belief, I began to think more critically about the people with whom I spent the most time.

What can I do to change?

(BEHAVIOR)

This question is extremely important because it helped me to see that, no matter how dim my situation may appear, it is within my power to change my circumstances. Recognizing my power, I felt the need to think critically about possible outcomes before making decisions. It also helped me to separate my actions from my being. Just because I failed a task does not make me a failure. With this understanding I witnessed a new sense of empowerment knowing I could seek, learn, and apply a specific set of behaviors to accomplish any goal I desire.

To whom/what should I change?

(GOALS AND OUTCOMES)

It was not enough to know I wanted to change. I needed to know to whom or what I wanted to change. This question challenged me to take a more critical look at the people and the world around me. I began taking inventory like I was shopping. If I saw a woman with excellent posture, I would take note of what to do. If I saw someone with a lifestyle or reputation I did not like, I would take note of what *not* to do. I used all of these findings to create my very own lifestyle and persona.

My personal results were astonishing; however, they were just that, *Personal* results. I questioned how this information would be received by industry professionals; however, while listening in on one of Dr. Chike Akua's classes at Clark Atlanta University, he mentioned the term "auto ethnography," which is a form of qualitative research in which an author uses self-reflection and writing to explore personal experience and connect it to wider cultural, political, and social meanings and understandings. This brings me back to my confession. Although I started this journey for my personal development, achieving Emotional Success was the deepest feeling of satisfaction I had ever experienced, and I wanted to share this with the world.

I began to wonder how my life would have been different if I had received this information and these tools sooner. What if there was a safe space for me to turn when I was coping with the effects of my sexual assault? What if there was a program that taught me confidence like my schoolteachers taught math and reading?

I made it my mission to create an organization to provide everything I needed when I was a girl. Through programs, presentations, and books – like this one – we are sharing the Social Emotional Learning techniques to make Emotional Success a common occurrence. Thank you in advance for taking the time to read this book. Please pay it forward and share these tools with everyone you know.

And with that...

7 Secrets to Social Emotional Learning

Enjoy. 😊

Secret #1

EQ Makes the Difference

In general, I find that many people are familiar with the concept of Intelligence Quotient (IQ) but there is still quite a bit of confusion surrounding Emotional Quotient (EQ.) Your IQ is associated with your intellect and matters of the brain while your EQ is associated with your feelings, emotions, and matters of your heart.

As a Social Emotional Learning (SEL) specialist, I have made it my mission to educate individuals on the significance of EQ and to provide them the tools needed to incorporate SEL into our education system, work environment, and everyday lives.

I was speaking with an educator at an alternative school about incorporating SEL practices in her school. She saw the value but was reluctant, stating, "I think this program would be great but we have to focus on preparing our students for testing. We are underperforming academically so I won't have the time to incorporate this type of program." I explained to her that incorporating an effective SEL program school wide would not only improve test scores, academics, and decrease behavior referrals, but also produce more well-rounded college and career ready graduates. She asked me to send her some information and I never heard from her again.

Set up for Failure

That woman did not mean any harm toward the students she serves. She just didn't know. She is simply following along with the practice of traditional education that tends to put heavier emphasis on academics as opposed to the soft skills needed to excel in life. If we continue on this path, we will continue to fail our students like the system failed a young Black male by the name of Rwenshaun "Shaun" Miller.

Shaun and I have been close friends since we were teenagers. We've always held each other accountable and challenged each other to succeed. When we were in high school, I was not the strongest student academically. I admired Shaun's ability to excel in multiple sports including basketball, football, and track while maintaining a 4.0 grade point average. He participated in clubs at school and always kept a positive spirit. He graduated high school and went to college at UNC Chapel Hill.

As we began both seeing success in our careers, I told Shaun that he needed to write a book to tell his story. As I helped him with the contents of his book, I felt like I was reading the story of a stranger.
I learned that when Shaun went off to college, he began dealing with some major mental health issues that led to confusion in his life. He began hearing voices. There were periods of time where he would go weeks without eating or sleeping. He became withdrawn and antisocial. Fortunately, his family decided to intervene and had him committed to the hospital. At the age of 20, Shaun was diagnosed with Bipolar Disorder and initially he did not know how to handle the news about his mental health. In the Black community, mental health is rarely

discussed and prioritized. In his book, *Injured Reserve*, he recounts the moment he was sitting in his car and pulled a gun to his head, and the only reason he is alive to share this story is because his gun jammed. This was not the Shaun I knew because his story did not match the outward expression of the Shaun everyone had grown to know and love.

How is your school measuring emotional deficiencies to prevent students like Shaun from slipping through the cracks? According to the "data," the school system would pat themselves on the back and say, "We've graduated this young Black male with a 4.0 GPA! Job well done!" However, what good is it to graduate your students if they act on self-harming thoughts when they go away to college? What good is it to cultivate scholars if they lack the appropriate skills needed to function socially and emotionally when they enter the real world? How many of you know a student like Shaun? How are they doing mentally and emotionally? Do you know?

One of the major challenges with traditional education process is we focus on developing our brain (IQ) at the expense of our hearts (EQ) when true success comes from developing IQ and EQ simultaneously.

True Success comes from developing IQ and EQ simultaneously.

Due to Shaun's commitment to his personal development journey and emotional resilience, he was able to achieve Emotional Success. Today Shaun is a Licensed Professional Counselor Associate, Mental Health Awareness Advocate, and the Founder of Eustress Inc. an organization geared toward removing the negative stigma about mental health in the Black community. The system failed Shaun because he deserved a holistic approach to his developmental process when was in grade school.

The Turning Point

Like Shaun's, every success story has a turning point. Some turning points happen as a result of an extremely low point in a person's life. Some turning points occur because of a positive influence. There are countless variations of success stories, but the turning points are most **always** EQ related.

There is an overwhelming amount of research that proves emotions drive our actions. If you look at a student who has demonstrated significant academic or behavioral growth, it typically isn't due to the student making a conscious decision to learn for the sake of learning. These types of gains are often made as a result of a meaningful relationship between a student and an educator, students' ability to relate what they are learning to a greater purpose that transcends the walls of the classroom, or their peers have influenced them to step it up. Although all the scenarios resulted in academic improvement,

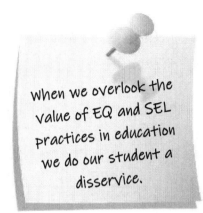

when we overlook the value of EQ and SEL practices in education we do our student a disservice.

all the turning points were EQ related. To overlook the value of EQ and SEL practices in education, we are missing out on tremendous opportunities and doing our students a disservice.

DIALOGUE

With one or more of your colleagues, use the following questions as conversation starters. Jot down anything you find useful or interesting.

1. Think of at least one student who made great gains during your time together. What were some of the factors involved in the turn around?

2. Making time to incorporate SEL programs in underperforming schools can help increase student achievement. Do you agree? Why or why not?

3. If your school is unable or unwilling to incorporate a schoolwide SEL program, what are some ways you can incorporate SEL practices in your role?

Secret #2

Stop Spreading Emotional Dysfunction

Before you enter this chapter, I want you to close your eyes for 15-30 seconds and think about the word "Emotions." What comes to mind?

When I do this activity with educators in professional learning settings, the responses are always pretty similar. I have heard some of the following responses:
"Drama"
 "Too emotional"
"Crying"
"I think of my female students."
"Hormones"
"They are bad or negative."

When we stop treating emotions like the plague, we will truly unlock the potential of our students, our schools and our community.

If this is what people are thinking about emotions, then there's no wonder why most educators try to stay as far away from that "emotional junk" as they can. There is a plethora of evidence-based data to support the holistic benefit of improving emotional intelligence and emotional literacy. When we stop treating emotions like the plague, we will truly unlock the potential of our students, our schools, and the community.

The solution to eradicating Emotional Dysfunction is to understand two core concepts: **You can't control emotions and you can't quantify emotions.** There are deep-rooted beliefs and habits that we must challenge as educators and there are new approaches for us to share with our students, but, most importantly, we have to model emotional intelligence for those around us. We will cover a few tools in this chapter, but don't stop here. Get as creative as you can while thinking of innovative ways to change the narrative around emotions in your schools and community.

You can't control your emotions

Countless times I have heard educators scream at students, "Control your emotions!" not realizing the complexity in such a seemingly simple request. See chart below to review healthier alternatives to decreasing the spread of emotional dysfunctional.

Dysfunctional	Healthier Approach
"Stop Crying"	"What happened, do you want to talk about it?"
"Get Out of Your Feelings"	"Do you feel up to writing out how you are feeling?"
"It's not that serious!"	"I see this is very important to you."
"Don't be Upset."	"It's okay to be upset."
"Calm Down."	"Do you need a minute to gather yourself?"

If something made me angry, then most likely I was

triggered by an internal or external stimulus. A person's triggers are like a defense mechanism or alarm system for their brain. Let's use two students as an example: a young girl by the name Jill and young boy named Jack who both have been determined to have behavior problems.

Jill behaves erratically anytime she has to meet with her male counselor. Her behavior is assumed to be problematic. However, upon further examination, we learn that she was raped by a man when she was a small child and being alone in a room with her male counselor triggers her to lash out as an attempt to protect herself and get out of that situation.

Jack was bullied at school, which caused him to feel embarrassed every day. However, when his family transferred him to a new school, he had hopes of starting over and making a new name for himself. On his first day, someone makes a joke about something he is wearing, and the entire class erupts into laughter. His brain remembers the embarrassment of his past and triggers him to fight the student who initiated the joke.

If we were to demand either of these students to "control their emotions," we would be telling Jack that he is wrong for feeling embarrassed and telling Jill that she should not feel scared. Educators must teach students the balance of honoring their emotions and learning how to display appropriate behavior by assisting our students with how to handle emotions like embarrassment, fear, anger, or any other emotions that may result in counterproductive behavior. The best way truly to assist our students with managing their emotions is to build a relationship, learn their triggers, and help them practice relevant strategies to effectively manage their behavior as triggers and emotions arise.

Keys to helping students manage their emotions:
- build a relationship,
- learn their triggers,
- practice relevant strategies to manage behavior

You Can't Quantify Emotions

"Oh my God Tierica, you're so emotional!" was something I heard so often growing up that I began to think it was a negative trait or a weakness. I believed I needed to toughen up and that's what I did. I did everything in my power to detach from my emotional side. Anytime I felt the urge to cry I would fight the urge and suppress my feelings. I would avoid getting too excited, too sad, or too emotional about anything. This is how I began my habit of Emotional Suppression.

Emotional Suppression is a coping mechanism used to manage the outward expression of one's feelings. Emotional Suppression can be tremendously dangerous mentally and physically. Studies show that emotional suppression and stress are major contributors to physical ailments and common illnesses.

Emotional Suppression is like blowing air into a balloon. Imagine that every time you experience an emotion with which you cannot deal you blow air into a balloon and try to forget that it's there. The emotions do not go away, they are taking up space in this balloon. However, there is only so much space in this balloon. When the balloon has reached capacity, what happens? *POP!* This "pop" is often exhibited as an overreaction to a situation, explosion, unexplained sadness, or other emotional response that does not seem appropriate for that particular situation.
"I don't know why that made me so angry."

Rwenshaun Miller of Eustress Inc. coined the phrase, "You can't quantify emotions." The problem is not that your students are furious or that they are extremely sad or excited. The issue is how they choose to react to these intense emotions. To tell students they are too emotional is to tell them they are wrong for feeling the way they feel and they should somehow dial it back, which often results in emotional suppression. A healthier alternative is to provide real time coping mechanisms to help your students manage reactions and behaviors.

Here are some tools you can share to change the narrative around emotions:
- **Honor your emotions**
  Have your students start by figuring out what they

are actually feeling. In some cases, students may disguise their scared emotion with anger and rage. This is called Emotional Substitution. It is important to create a culture and climate that give them permission to honor their authentic emotions.

- **Find constructive ways to express emotions**
  Honoring authentic emotions does not give students permission to run amuck. Remind your students during this process that their emotions do NOT excuse their actions! It's okay to feel angry but that does not give anyone a free pass to punch someone in the face. Finding constructive ways to express emotions is essential to self-mastery. It takes a great level of maturity for a student to feel angry, honor those emotions, and demonstrate impulse control.

- **Source your emotions**
  Get your students in the habit of asking themselves from where are these emotions coming? Is it my current situation? Could some of the emotions be coming from something that may have happened last week, last year, or maybe from my childhood? Helping students gain clarity on the source of their emotions may help identify their triggers and find new ways to constructively express their emotions.

- **Get what you need**
  When individuals learn to source their emotions effectively, they will start to see that there are messages in their feelings. These messages are

designed to help individuals get what they need whether it is support, reassurance, boundaries, or maybe just need some sleep. Like any other skill, your students will get better the more they practice with the right tools. This tool is known as Feelings as Messengers. This concept was shared with me by my counselors Wekesa and Afiya Madzimoyo and it completely blew my mind! For a deeper dive into this paradigm shifting concept visit AyaEd.com.

- **Feed Your Emotions**
  Imagine you have two fires burning at the same time; as they both start to burn out, you begin throwing logs on one fire and it grows bigger, brighter, and hotter while the other fire burns down to ashes. Now imagine one of those fires represents depression and the other fire represents joy. Often, your emotions work the same way. You have the power to choose which emotion you will feed, and which emotion will burn down to ashes.

How do you feed your emotions? You can feed your emotions in many ways. Here is a short list of ways we feed our emotions every day:

- Movies
- Television
- Reading
- Music
- Exercise/Sports
- Massages
- The people around you
- Mentors/Coaches
- Experiences
- Self-Talk

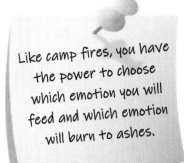

Like camp fires, you have the power to choose which emotion you will feed and which emotion will burn to ashes.

Pay attention to the emotions you are experiencing. If you want to experience more of a particular emotion, like clarity, think of what you've been doing that may have brought you clarity, like running, listening to a particular song, meditating, or a conversation with a family member. Whatever it is, do it more often.

If you find that an undesirable emotion is reoccurring, like frustration, try to find the source of that emotion and limit those actions or experiences. Maybe we need to decrease the conversation time with the Negative Nancy's in our life or avoid waiting until the last minute to complete a task. In some cases, you may not have a choice, like going to work or doing laundry. Our students experience this as well when it comes to going to school, doing homework, and chores. In these situations, we have to put in the time to do what we have to do so we can get back to throwing logs on the other fire.

For example, when I find myself being more snappy, aggressive, or confrontational, I listen to less aggressive music. I try to listen to more neo soul or R&B because I know the music to which I listen directly impacts my mood. I am not telling you that watching your favorite show or listening to your favorite music is bad, just pay attention to your mood, emotions, and attitude and adjust where necessary. These adjustments can be temporary or permanent.

Learn, Practice, Share!

It's important for us to change the narrative around EQ by learning as much as we can about emotions, tools, and strategies because it will help us to develop our mental and emotional health. Learning to manage and master your emotions is an essential part of our emotional heath. Healthy trees bear healthier fruit. Put the tools you learn to use and share what works for you with others.

Healthy trees bear healthier fruit.

Share!

The last idea we'll cover in this chapter may sound simple, but it is the hardest thing for some people to do. Just the act of sharing your feelings, experiences, triggers, and your story will inspire others to do the same. There are so many ways to share, just find the way that best fits your personality.

Various ways to share:
- Join a support group
- Write a book
- Journal
- Start a blog
- Start an awareness movement/organization
- Express yourself through the arts
- You can even share anonymously

Write

Write down as many dysfunctional beliefs, practices, and statements that you can remember. Next, write what makes it dysfunctional and a more functional, alternative approach.

(If you need more space, use the notes section in the back of this book)

Emotional Dysfunction	Why is it Dysfunctional	Alternative Approach

Secret #3

Social Awareness

you can understand the emotions, needs, and concerns of other people, pick up on emotional cues, feel comfortable socially, and recognize the power dynamics in a group or organization.

While SEL requires a large amount of personal development and discovery, social interactions play an important role in one's emotional intelligence. Cultural Sensitivity, empathy, love, boundaries, communication, respect, and social awareness are a few of the many ways we practice EQ with others. Whether you are teaching this information to your students or using these skills to develop your own EQ, here are a few basic rules to remember.

Communication is Paramount
I challenge anyone to come up with a more important aspect of any relationship than communication — more important than trust, love, respect, empathy, and even boundaries. Communication is the most important because it is the only way to make the other person(s) in the relationship aware of these other aspects. As important as it is, there is not enough time spent on equipping our students with effective communication skills at an early age. Training our students how to read body language, say what you mean, be an active listener, and articulate your words will take them a long way. If our students do not receive these basic skills before they reach adulthood, they will be ill equipped to navigate relationships successfully at work, in their personal lives, and day to day interactions. Help your students understand that we are always communicating even when we are not conscious of it. We communicate through our words, facial expressions, body language, attire, hair styles, jewelry, actions, and even our silence! This may not be something they master during their time with you but plant the seeds and help them understand that constant development is needed to effectively connect with those around us.

World Views are like fingerprints

Like fingerprints, World Views are unique to each individual. While you may share similar perspectives on many topics, there are no two individuals who have the same perspective, idea, and opinion on every topic. That's because our experiences color the lenses through which we see the world. That's why even identical twins growing up in the same household can have differing views on life because individually they have had unique experiences that will ultimately shape their views and opinions on the world.

World Views are like fingerprints they are unique to each individual.

-Tierica Berry

Having differing views in your classrooms and school buildings is not a bad thing, in my opinion it is what makes life more interesting. The challenge comes when individuals are unable to respect a narrative that challenges their own.

As educators, we encounter students from all walks of life. Some of them may come from families with world views that may challenge what we believe. It is not our job to make them believe what we believe or to make them stop believing in that which they believe. Our job is simply to educate them and provide them with the knowledge, skills, and tools to be the best version of themselves no matter their racial, cultural, sexual, religious, or political background.

This requires us being open to accepting different narratives even if we don't agree. You may not agree with the political views of a student, but it is important that you remain open and accept that his/her views have been shaped through experiences. An elderly white woman will likely have different experiences than an African American male raised in the inner city. This may cause for a disconnect in their views, but the disconnect does not make either of their realities any less valid. In the words of Steven R. Covey,

"We see the world not as it is but as we are."
7 Habits of Highly Effective People

Code Switching

I had a white woman approach me at a conference. She asked me for some advice on how to get African American students to stop using improper English. I told her that the best way to get buy in from her students on "proper English" is to avoid referring to the way they speak currently as bad or wrong. When we, as educators, tell our students the way they are speaking is bad or wrong then we run the risk of offending their family norms. "Teacher, my entire family talks like this. If you are saying the way I speak is **wrong,** then you are saying my entire family is **wrong!** Now you have lost my respect!"

Students Have Triggers, Too!

When dealing with emotions, we spend a significant amount of time on learning and managing our triggers and teach our young people to do the same. I have seen people become so self-aware that they begin to negate their social awareness. There are many components of social awareness, but this one hits home for me because I have experienced it first hand on the giving and receiving end. One of my triggers is being ignored. As I became more self-aware, I began sharing my trigger with others. Because I shared this information with my fiancé when we began dating, I felt I had a pass to assert myself when I felt I was being ignored. I recall a disagreement we had that resulted in him needing to take a moment to clear his head. I interpreted that as him ignoring me and I began asserting myself demanding attention. After all, he knew that ignoring me was one of my triggers. What I failed to appreciate is that by asserting myself without taking his triggers into consideration, I was selfishly triggering them and driving a wedge in our relationship.

Get Creative!

Ditch the traditional teaching methods! Without using textbooks, lectures, or instructional videos, come up with 4 interactive activities that would allow your students to learn and/or practice Social Awareness.

1.
2.
3.
4.

Secret #4

Processing Emotional Trauma

A large underlying issue with Social Emotional development is the lack of tools and guidance for individuals to process emotional trauma. Everyone experiences emotional trauma in different phases of life. While some experiences may be more traumatic than others, the same rules still apply. In order to exercise good habits that positively impact your students' mental health, it is imperative they have multiple outlets to process and cope with emotional trauma in a healthy way. In addition to seeing a therapist, victims of Emotional Trauma may benefit from a peer support group, an artistic outlet, and a safe space to express themselves freely. In order to help young people grasp this concept, I created an activity guide titled Unpacking the Emotional Suitcase.

An Emotional Suitcase is the place individuals store painful, embarrassing, or traumatic experiences, usually because they do not know how to or do not wish to process them. The guide is designed to walk students through processing their emotional trauma on their own or with the assistance of a counselor.

The most effective way to describe what we call, the Emotional Processing System *(illustrated in the diagram on the next page)* is to compare it to one's digestive system. If your digestive system is working properly, when you eat something, your body will store what it needs and get rid of what it doesn't. However, if your digestive system is not working properly, your body will store everything because it does not know how to process what you just ate. As a result, you become bloated, constipated, and you begin to see other symptoms occur. This is your body's indicator that there is something wrong.

Similar to our digestive system, our Emotional Processing System also has a way of letting us know when something is going wrong.

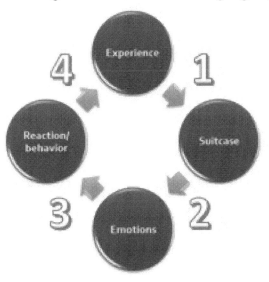

 Following the digestive system analogy, having an experience is the same as eating something. If we do not know how to process what we just experienced, then we shove everything into our emotional suitcase.

2 The problem is, when we shove those experiences in our emotional suitcase our emotions do not go away.

3 If we do not process what we are feeling these emotions will come back at some point. They will exhibit themselves in reactions and behaviors.

4 These behaviors leave us vulnerable for more negative experiences that we shove into our suitcase and this is how the viscous cycle of emotional suppress begins.

With a better understanding of the Emotional Processing System, we can get to the root of the problem to help our students reprocess their emotional trauma. We'll start by identifying reactions and behaviors, gaining access to emotions, facilitating student expression, and, finally, reprocessing emotional trauma.

Start with Reactions and Behaviors

When *Unpacking an Emotional Suitcase,* it is common to start by identifying the reactions and behaviors because it is what we can see. Actions serve as potential indicators for deeper issues. Some common indicators may include sexual promiscuity, drastic change in behavior, aggression, bullying, unexplained changes in mood, etc. These are just a few behaviors that may stem from Emotional Trauma.

Gain Access to Emotions

When working with your students to understand how they really feel, it is critically important to develop rapport with them and build authentic relationships. Failure to establish meaningful connections with students may result in very surface-only relationships, meaning no matter how hard you dig or what type of questions you ask, you will continue to get surface answers like, "good," "fine," and "I'm all right." Relationships may look different from one student to the next, but that is perfectly fine because no two students are the same.

Here are some practices that have been useful to myself and other educators across the country:

- Be authentic

- Open your Emotional Suitcase

- Follow through

- Give respect and trust

Facilitating the Expression Process

Before you can get a student to open up about personal matters, you have to create an environment that makes him/her feel safe enough to share these sensitive topics. Safe zones are important because it makes a person feel comfortable enough to open up freely. By developing safe spaces that honor individual privacy and authentic emotions, we create a culture and climate that becomes comfortable and trusted. After that culture and climate has been established, then the unpacking can begin.

Imagine you just had a student transfer into your class, school, or program. How will you know what the student has experienced? How will you learn his/her likes and dislikes? How will you learn the student's triggers? Every student comes with baggage, not just the ones who have been labeled "At-Risk." The only way to find out what is in that baggage is for him/her to unpack it through expression. Unpacking occurs in various forms of expression. Including but not limited to:

- Writing
- Talking
- Drawing
- Poetry
- Behavior
- Acting
- Singing
- Dancing
- Music

As a student, I wrote poetry in my spare time, but I hated writing in school because of all the rules. Focusing on doing it right overshadowed my ability to share my authentic feelings. We can learn so much about our students by building in time to lower rules and boundaries to allow them to express themselves freely.

I was having a conversation with a young lady I'd known since she was ten. I'd known her for about six years. At sixteen, her mother

43

told me she began acting out in school, displaying promiscuous behavior, being disrespectful to authority, using foul language, and her grades were slipping. After establishing a sense of trust with her, I was able to introduce the Unpacking the Emotional Suitcase Process to her and she said, "I have a lot of stuff in my emotional suitcase."

I responded, "Well you are too small to be carrying around all that baggage. Let's start unpacking." Although she had bought into the process of Unpacking her Emotional Suitcase, she was not a big talker. However, we agreed that I would help her write her first poem if she could write out her thoughts on paper. By the time we finished the process, I was able to learn about emotions she had been suppressing since long before we met. Creativity is one of the clearest windows to the soul and allowing individuals to be creative will give you a clearer view of their reality. It is the ultimate form of expression, making it the perfect tool for Unpacking Your Emotional Suitcase.

Creativity is one of the clearest windows to the soul.

Tierica B.

Help Reprocess Emotional Trauma

An unprocessed experience is any experience that is still closely associated with burdening emotions, like embarrassment, shame, resentment, guilt, etc. These are the heavy emotions that weigh down your Emotional Suitcase. Our students are walking into our classrooms with these heavy loads every day. The next activity is a great resource to help your students reprocess their Emotional Trauma. This will enable them to take a more empowered stance as it relates to their experiences, move from victim to survivor and turn their pain into power.

Reprocessing Activity

The Reprocessing Activity takes individuals through an exercise that prompts them to answer four questions regarding individual experiences. What? Why? How? And Now?

- **WHAT** is the traumatic experience? Go into as much detail as you can.
- **WHY** is hard to overcome? List any concerns, fears, thoughts, or other factors that make this experience difficult.
- **HOW** can I process this experience? Make a list of strategies and supports that may help me along your journey.
- **NOW** what?! How do I turn my pain to power? What can I take with me from this experience?

Once this activity has been completed, the key to reprocessing is going step by step through the items listed in the "Why" section.

These are barriers that are standing between you and emotional success. Let's practice with Monee's story.

Here is the poem Monee wrote as a result of our Emotional Suitcase conversation.

All my life I have been craving this affection, attention, and love.
Knowing that I would not be able to get it from my daddy
because he's smiling from up above.
Not having what I so badly needed caused all this pain.
I secretly hope that you my mother would change.
But instead you left me out in the rain.
Although it hurts and saddens me, I try to stay sane.
I desperately needed you especially when you left me with others.
But I know that I would never be able to change the fact that you're my mother.
I always felt that you put someone over me.
That mother that I needed, I know that you would never be.
You always wanted the credit for being there.
But every time I needed you, I asked the question where?
Where were you when I was down bad.
Keeping all these emotions in made me so sad.
No matter how I felt I never could stay mad at you.
Knowing that you did not receive what you needed too.

Monee' 2014

Reprocessing Example

What?	Why?
• The loss of her father. • Feelings of neglect/abandonment from her mother	• She is not getting the things she needs from her parents • The pain and sadness that comes with it.

How?	Now?
• Find other sources for attention, affection, and love. • Get maternal nurturing from another mother figure.	• Use writing as an outlet • Strive for success to inspire others in her situation.

When working through this process with Monee, we focused on the barriers that were making it difficult for her to process her life experiences. Taking them one by one, I helped her realize that although she was not getting the attention, affection, and love she believed she needed from her biological parents that she was still able to receive those things from her adopted parents that had taken her in as their own. Second, I stressed to her that there was nothing wrong with feeling pain and sadness about her situation. The important part was for her to honor her feelings and allow herself to feel them instead of numbing herself with boys and other vices. I gave her an assignment to find various forms of expression that honors who she is as a person and her authentic emotions. Monee is now a high school graduate and is traveling the world serving our country in the U.S. Navy.

Reprocess

Sharing this work as a concept you read in a book for professional development may be impactful, but when you share from a more personal place there is an increased level of passion and belief in that which you are sharing. Take a moment to complete the Reprocessing Activity with one of your own unprocessed experiences. If you need more space, use the notes pages in the back of this book.

- **WHAT** is the traumatic experience? Go into as much detail as you can.
- **WHY** is hard to overcome? List any concerns, fears, thoughts, or other factors that make this experience difficult.
- **HOW** can I process this experience? Make a list of strategies and supports that may help me along your journey.
- **NOW** what?! How do I turn my pain to power? What can I take with me from this experience? How can I use this with my students?

Reprocessing Activity

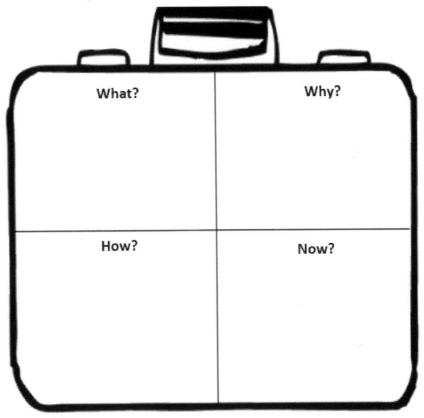

| What? | Why? |
| How? | Now? |

Secret #5

Be Trauma Responsive when it REALLY counts

Trauma Informed Care (TIC) is a holistic, person-centered approach to treatment that understands and incorporates the biological, psychological, neurological, and social impact of trauma on an individual (Lenape Valley Foundation, 2013). TIC is a buzz word in education and while we are raising awareness as an industry, there is still a great deal of development needed to prepare educators to be Trauma Responsive when it really counts. It is easy to be trauma responsive when we are in a training class acting out scenarios or when all the conditions line up just like we practiced or like the professional development books taught us. However, it is not as easy for me to be Trauma Responsive when I have been triggered, tension is high on both sides, and I have slipped into defensive mode. This is when being Trauma Responsive really counts!

I was raised on what we call "basic old school" principles, such as:

Yes, ma'am. No sir.

speak when you're spoken to

Don't talk back

Stay out of 'grown folks' business.

When we didn't abide by these "basic old school" principles, there were consequences and repercussions for our actions. But times have changed. Just a few of the major influencers that have changed the climate for our students in education include parental expectations and accountability, youth access to information is easier than ever before, and the high focus on standardized testing and rigorous academics. It is essential to keep these factors in mind when interacting with our students, especially in high-stress situations.

When in a group home as a house parent, one of my new residents was Little Miss Shy. We had just come in from our after-school pick up run and Shy disagreed with me about one of the basic house rules. She began shouting at me and even called me a B****. I did not allow that to upset me. In a calm voice, I reminded her that profanity is not allowed in this house nor will I tolerate being disrespected. She was expecting me to yell back at her, curse, catch an attitude, or be offended. When I did not give the response she was expecting, she became outraged! She lunged at me swinging and trying to hit me. Because I was trained in CPI and her actions had become a threat to me, her, and the safety of those around her I used a non-aggressive restraint technique that allowed her to calm down without causing any harm to herself or anyone else. During this time, I did NOT make condescending comments or threats. I did NOT antagonize her with petty jabs and emotional undercuts. I spoke as calmly as before, reminding her that when she was no longer a threat, I would let her go. I continued the say, "Shy, when you are ready, we can go sit on the couch and talk." She continued to kick and scream. I waited in silence. After a very short period I asked, "Shy, are you ready?" reluctantly said, "Yes." As promised, I let her go and asked her to have a seat on the couch. We discussed why she was so upset, and I told her that while living here there were many benefits to look forward to. However, there are also expectations to live up to. From that moment on, we had a wonderful relationship.

The reason this story is so relevant is because I took into consideration that Shy had been in several group homes before coming to us. I understand that her relationship with her parents involved a lot of yelling, profanity, and some abuse. Being trauma informed led me to being trauma responsive. I made a conscious choice not to belittle her for her actions and model the desired behavior to show her the culture and climate of this new home she had entered. After a while, I recall being able to give her what I call the "momma look" and she would quickly self-correct. Like most of our children Shy longed for structure, accountability, consistency, and to be loved despite her shortcomings.

Being called the B word or swung at by a child would trigger some adults to assert themselves to let the child know who's boss. I have even seen some antagonize the child with comments like, "oh you not so big now" or "now who's the B****?!" "That's why nobody wants you now!" Not only are you validating every negative thought they have about adults, you are also validating any insecurities they have about themselves and the value they bring to the world.

In order to be trauma responsive with our students when it really counts, we must remember to take into consideration their past experiences with adults regarding trust, reliability, discipline, and love.

Here are a few ways to remain Trauma Responsive when it REALLY counts:

Check your baggage at the door

It sounds good and it is always easier said than done because we have baggage, too. There are situations we have not processed and issues we still need to work through. Some of our emotional triggers can be more difficult to manage than others. But it is important that we get into the habit of checking our baggage at the door for your sake and for the sake of the children. If you bring unprocessed baggage into the classroom, your students will pick up on that and some of them may attempt to use it against you. I remember one of my teachers brought some of his family baggage to school one day and the students know from that moment forward what they needed to do to press his buttons.

If you have emotional baggage that you fear may impede your effective functioning in your professional or personal life, please order a copy of Unpacking the Emotional Suitcase from our website and work through that book as soon as possible. It may be helpful to go through this process with an accountability partner, counselor, or therapist.

Remember: It's not about you

"I HATE YOU!"

I've learned that if a student plays this card or begins teasing us, it often has less to do with us than we think. Some of the reasons students may have to play these cards include:

- To distract from poor academic ability
- To stop you from getting to close
- To protect themselves from going to deep with you emotionally
- Your appearance, voice, scent, etc., may trigger memories from a past aggressor
- This is how they interact with their family members

This list is endless. If this has ever been an issue for you before, I hope this section comes to mind to help relieve a little pressure in those situations. Just take a step back and remember, "This is not about me."

don't let pride get in the way
Think win-win -Steven Covey
surrender the one up - Chrisitian Moore

If the goal is truly to help our children heal from past trauma, then we must not allow our own baggage to get in the way. Practicing how we should respond when tension is high will enable us to be better prepared to handle these situations when they arise.

Reflect

Be Trauma Responsive When It REALLY Counts

To be successful with this secret requires planning and being proactive. High stress and highly tense situations typically show a person's true character. Your ability to remain composed and still demonstrate empathy and care for your students is the key.

1. Reflect on a time when you saw a coworker in a tense or stressful situation where they may have lost their composure and displayed a lack of empathy for the student(s) they were working with. Write down the story as it happened.

2. How could that scenario played out if the person was able to remain trauma responsive in this situation? Rewrite the story using your trauma responsive techniques.

3. Repeat steps 1 and 2 using a story of your own.

Secret #6

Refocus
Opportunities

Refocus
Verb
To adjust the attention or resources

on something new or different.

When we break down the term refocus to its simplest definition, it can help us be more intentional about the opportunities we have to literally refocus our students' attention to more desirable behaviors and outcomes. In many cases, our students' energy, attention, and resources are directed toward short-term objectives that may derail them from the bigger picture. For example, some of your students may feel they do not have a voice at home so when they come to school they want to be heard. They do not want to be taken advantage of so, their objective is to be as loud as they can and to interject wherever they see fit, with no consideration for anyone else's voice or feelings. Continuing on this path may lead to challenges forming healthy relationships or receiving a quality education. This could also lead to other behavioral challenges and a long record of behavior referrals. There are many creative ways to refocus this student's energy in a constructive manner that honors his/her emotions and still allows him to feel heard and important. It is important to build relationships and get to know your students to learn what their goals and objectives are.

Debriefing after occurrences

Recidivism is a major challenge in our society. There have been several initiatives in schools to help reduce the recidivism rates on discipline referrals, suspensions, and expulsions. One seemingly small practice I saw in a school in Las Vegas, NV, is paying off in a big way. The principal at this junior high school is very intentional about using "Refocus Meetings" to debrief after occurrences. Her belief is that when a student is suspended for an infraction, such as fighting, the student returns with the same mindset with which he/she left. This will only set the student up to reoffend in the future. She created a process that requires students to write the statement on what happened and return with a parent for a meeting. Some of the members of the admin staff would sit down with all parties involved to discuss what happened and how we can prevent this situation from happening again. While this may not stop all discipline referrals, she has seen a decrease in her recidivism rate.

If your school has not implemented refocus meetings schoolwide, then start with your students. Create your own refocus meeting process and document the results. Here are a few things to remember during implementation:

- Send them home with something to reflect on during their suspension. Communicate to them they will be expected to discuss with you upon their return.

- Will you require parents to attend these meetings? In some cases, this may be harder than others. Learn your demographics and the family dynamics of your students.

- Set your objectives for the debriefs but remain agile. You may have in your mind that the meeting will follow a standard agenda, but if new information comes out that requires a different level of attention or time, remain agile and prepared for anything.

- Debriefing outside of the stress response helps parties return to the table with a leveled head. Sometimes your stress response may have been triggered. Be sure to debrief outside of your stress response as well.

Document your results on this progress and make adjustments where necessary. With the right turn around, this may be something that become a schoolwide or districtwide initiative.

Strength-based approach

I have always been a talker. I love the act of expressing myself through language and making connections with people. As an adult, I have leveraged these skills as a professional speaker to build my own business. However, when I was in school, most of my teachers were not fans of my talkative nature. My progress reports would often read, "very bright but too talkative!" "Social Butterfly," "Tierica Talks too much!" It got to a point where I would apologize, "Sorry, I talk a lot." Most of my teachers taught me at a young age that talking was negative. How could something I loved to do so much be so bad? I must be a bad person.

My 9th grade math teacher, Mr. Goings, helped me to see my talkative nature in a different light. I would breeze through my work before my peers. There was nothing left for me to do but TALK! Mr. Goings noticed that I was distracting others from completing their work. Instead of chastising me, he pulled me to the side and asked me to jump ahead to the next lesson because he wanted me to teach the class the next day. I was so excited! *"I get to stand in front of the class, be the center of attention, and not get in trouble for it? YES!"* He refocused my talking to student teaching and peer mentorship for the remainder of the year. Honestly, Mr. Goings' efforts are part of the reason I am able to stand in front of audiences today.

Although some behaviors our students display may test our patience, we must make a conscious effort to honor student strengths and refocus their attention and energy toward a constructive objective. You could be the catalyst in your student's life that plants the seed of entrepreneurship, public speaking, or leadership.

Active Listening

I had just received information that someone had lost a loved one to senseless gun violence. I have learned that my stress response is to go into fix it mode. As I am listening to someone speak, my mind automatically is scanning the conversation for solutions, solace, and support. Because I knew this was a delicate situation and I did not want to do more harm than good, I called my therapist for some guidance on how to best support this individual in her time of need. His exact words were, "Leave your Fix-it Hat at home and just listen." I was instructed to allow her the space to honor her feelings and not try to rush her back to "happy." She's going to be angry, and that's okay. She may cry and that's fine, too. What I gathered from that conversation is that no matter how noble my intentions may be, at that moment my most important duty was to just listen. Can you relate? This is an important part of the refocus opportunities because students are going to be less likely to buy into your guidance if they do not feel heard. Practicing active listening can work in your favor when it comes to refocusing students.

There are many aspects of active listening, all of which have their own time and place. There are conversations where we may practice active listening and it is appropriate to provide solutions and other times it is not. There are times where you can share a relatable story and sometimes you should just allow space for the person speaking to share his/her truth. One of the simplest ways to gain clarity on what type of conversation it should be is simply to ask. "would you like my advice or do you just want me to listen?" or any other variation of this question. Here are a few rules of thumb to practicing active listening.

- **Don't fill the air**
  Some people are extremely uncomfortable with silence. If you are that person, try not to fill the air by talking too much! There is a big difference between saying something meaningful and talking for the sake of talking. When having personal conversations with your students, think critically about your words and the advice you give. Ask yourself if what you are sharing will benefit the situation. If the answer is not "yes," then let it go.

- **Silence is golden...maybe**
  Let's say you have mastered the "don't fill the air" skill but your student is the one who does not feel comfortable with silence. You can learn this by simply asking, "are you okay with silence?" Offer some non-invasive background

options like non-vocal background music or whatever may be appropriate for your setting. Another dynamic I have seen is the student feeling like they have an obligation to fill the air for us. In that case, I let them know that we can talk or just sit her quietly to reflect. Whichever you prefer. Just don't feel obligated either way.

- **Request Clarity**
Paraphrasing and requesting clarity can be helpful for you to get a better understanding of what is being communicated and make the student feel you really care. Even using active listening cues like hmm, wow, okay and appropriate facial expressions could help with this as well. Whatever you do, make it authentic. These questions and listening cues should not sound forced or rehearsed.

- **Giving your Undivided attention**
You can show your students they have your undivided attention by eliminating distractions, demonstrating attentive posture and body language, and maintaining casual eye contact. I say casual eye contact because if you are staring at them like they are in an interrogation session, it may make the conversation a little uncomfortable. Also, if a distraction happens to arise, clearly communicate what is about to happen and apologize for the interruption. "Excuse me, I apologize for the interruption. My daughter's school has called 3 times. Do you mind if I take this call? As soon as I finish, we can pick up right where we left off." Another step I like to take is to repeat the last thing I heard them say. "You were telling me about when you and your mother went to the store last week. We'll pick up there, don't forget what you were going to say!" And when you return from your interruption remember to pick up right there.

- **Listen to what is NOT being said**
  According to professor Albert Mehrabian's book, *Silent Messages*, only 7% of our communication is verbal (Mehrabian, 2007). Therefore, in addition to what is being communicated verbally, we must be able to interpret tone of voice and body language or we could miss most of the messages being communicated. If your student is sitting with arms folded, he/she may be uncomfortable or may be cold. If you lean in and your student leans back, the student may be communicating they are uncomfortable with your proximity. Pay close attention and, when in doubt...ASK FOR CLARITY!

- **Increase Your emotional literacy**
  Have you ever heard someone say, "you don't understand how I feel!" Increasing your emotional literacy will help you be more attuned to the wide array of emotions that your students may be feeling on a day-to-day basis. Study your own feelings and the feelings of others. Ask questions, dig deeper if the student is comfortable with sharing. This will boost your emotional literacy making you more relatable and more valuable during these types of conversations.

- **Don't rush students back to "happy"**
  It is only natural to want your students to feel good and be happy; but, unfortunately, that will not always be the case. Saying things like "don't worry" or "don't be sad" is not always the answer. Sometimes students need a safe place for their anger, pain, and frustration to be expressed and heard. If you spend that time trying to get them to look at the bright side of things, students may leave feeling like their emotions are not important. To avoid that scenario, take the time to acknowledge their emotions with affirming statements like, "It's okay to be angry" or "Crying can be therapeutic."

Allowing your students to take their time to process their feelings can strengthen your relationship with them and demonstrate active listening.

Choices

When we are refocusing our students, the goal should be for them eventually to be able to self-regulate and refocus themselves. A powerful part of that is student choice.

"Because I said so!"
   "It's my way or the highway!"

This dogmatic approach does not serve our students well. As a matter of fact, in many ways this is setting them up for failure. When we strip our education process of any opportunities for student choice and student voice, then we rob our students of the opportunity to think critically.

When children are given options, they exercise their power to choose. They become confident in their ability to make sound decisions. Practicing problem solving teaches them to trust their own critical thinking process. Another added benefit is it helps shift the mindset of students who suffer from a general sense of helplessness. These students typically believe they have no control over the outcomes in their lives, they may believe adults are responsible for everything and they must accept whatever life throws at them. Giving these students options whenever possible could literally change the trajectory of their entire life! The power of choice cannot be understated. It teaches our students that each person has the power to choose the direction of his/her life, that most of the outcomes we experience in our lives are based on the decisions we have made, and that we are more in control than we think.

I want to be clear: giving your students options to choose does not mean that your expectations are optional. It is important to let students know which expectations and routines are flexible and which are not. Being explicit about why certain rules are nonnegotiable helps your students with logic and reason. It also helps increase the probability of them abiding by those rules.

When students walk into Ms. Clinton's class, they are expected to enter quietly, choose among one of three assignment options, and begin immediately. Ms. Clinton believes that incorporating opportunities for student choice throughout the day will help students to be more confident in their own decision-making process. While giving them choices, she does not compromise her expectations that every student will enter class quietly and get to work immediately. Take a moment and review your routine and expectations. Where can you build in options for students to exercise their decision-making skills and power of choice? Ask your students for ideas on how to deliver upcoming lessons and instruction. This will create more buy in and boost student morale.

Plan of Action

Working in the field of education and in the school system, there will be conflict. There is no way around it. The question is how do we manage conflict in such a way that it does not reoccur? Creating your own refocus process to address conflict as it arises can help to reduce the rate repeat occurrences. With your role, students, and demographics in mind, plan out a refocus/debriefing plan you can implement to address occurrences. Use the examples and lessons provided in this chapter to customize a process that fits your specific needs.

The ideal plan would:

- Have a simple and easy to remember plan name
- Outline clear and concise steps and expectations
- incorporate a mix of proactive and reactive practices to address a wide array of situations.

Plan Name:

Secret #7

Beliefs: The Glue that Holds it all Together

With Social and Emotional Development and any other development process, one's **belief system** is one of the most important contributors to sustainable success. I knew that beliefs were important, but the true paradigm shift came from the Outcome Progression Model (OPM) introduced to me by one of my earlier mentors. Using this information, educators across the country have been able to see how behavior referrals, academic performance, and many other outcomes follow this model (Hotep 2012).

The Outcome Progression Model
by Hotep, Educational Success Strategist

Outcomes

Behavior

Decisions

Belief System

Teachings/ Upbringing

Copyright 2012 Hustle U Inc.

Your students' outcomes are arrived at based on their behavior. Their behavior is based on their decisions. Every decision they make is based on their belief system, and their belief system is developed from their teaching and upbringing.

While administering a creative writing program at a Youth Detention Center in Florida, my team began a discussion that prompted participants to share why they act out. A young lady stood to her feet with all the confidence in the world and shared, "Because if I don't act out... I don't get no attention!" About 90% of the girls in the room began to nod their head in agreement.

I was in awe! These girls told me that they were incarcerated (Outcome) because they engaged in illegal activity (behavior) based on a conscious

(Decision) to act out. This decision was based on the belief that, "If I don't act out, I won't get any attention." (belief system) This belief system was established based on repetitive demonstrations at school and at home (Teaching and Upbringing.)

The OPM is playing out right before our eyes every day! Our traditional discipline program is missing the mark completely! We have been telling these girls to, "Stop fighting and you won't get suspended! Stop fighting and you won't get expelled! Stop fighting and you won't go to jail!" This method focuses all our attention, energy, and resources on the behavior and outcomes. But behavior and outcomes are only the tip of the iceberg! The red line in the model represents the surface. Like the iceberg, everything above the line you can see but there is much more beneath the surface. Allow me to walk you through how our behavior problems are much deeper than they appear.

The Outcome Progression Model

by Hotep, Educational Success Strategist

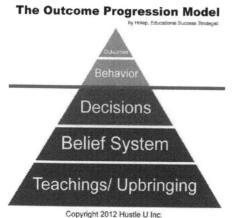

Incarceration

"Acting out" Fighting/illegal activity

Decided to act out for attention

If I don't act out, I won't get attention

This fact was demonstrated and reinforced

Copyright 2012 Hustle U Inc.

What those girls taught me that day is our students are making a conscious decision to behave or misbehave. During our professional development series, we deliver an entire workshop to help educators see how this dynamic is at play every day in their classrooms and school buildings. As educators, we have all had conversations with students about fighting. Their response is typically that they understand and they won't do it again, but next week what happens? They're fighting again! The conversation we had with that student did not promote sustainable change because we are focusing our attention on the behaviors and outcomes, but the problem is much deeper than that. The most effective way to sustainably change student outcomes is not to focus on behaviors, but to focus on beliefs. If you want to see a change in academics, fighting, dress code, teen pregnancy, suicide, or any other outcome, invest more time in addressing dysfunctional beliefs and replacing them with functional beliefs to see a positive impact on those behaviors.

Addressing Dysfunctional Belief Systems

The Outcome Progression Model is an excellent tool to assist with identifying dysfunctional belief systems. But, once we have identified them, what is the next step? How do we put this information to use?

Below are four questions that will help transform dysfunctional belief systems. Depending on your position, workload, and interaction with the students, implementation of this process may vary. It will take creativity and the ability to think outside the box.

1. How do we learn what our students believe?
2. What do our students believe?
3. What are some ways to change dysfunctional beliefs?
4. What are some functional beliefs that could lead to more productive behavior?

How do we learn what our students believe?

We have to start by gaining access to what our students believe. Sometimes you will learn their beliefs through casual conversation. There are some belief systems that may not be as openly accessible. Here are some ways to access what students believe:

- Hold classroom meetings/discussions on current events.
- Assign writing prompts where students can express. themselves freely without the pressure of being graded for grammar, spelling, and punctuation. These limitations can stunt the creativity and freedom of expression.
- Build a role-playing scenario around relevant topics.
- Any form of artistic expression. You can learn a lot by allowing your students to choose their favorite form of artistic expression. *(poetry, drawing, painting, lyricsm, vision boards, or singing)*

When conducting these activities, hopefully students will feel comfortable opening up. In some cases, they may share deeply personal information. Be sure to cover your mandatory reporting guidelines with your students *BEFORE* they begin. try to share the guidelines in a way that communicates that you care about getting them out of compromising situations.

What do our students believe?

Once you develop vehicles for expression, the second question is designed to help you develop a clear picture of what your students believe. You will have to be observant and sometimes read between the lines. Some beliefs will be very clear, for others you may have to dig a little by asking probing questions. Be sure not to make the students feel as if they are being interrogated. Some noninvasive probing could be, "what do you mean by that?" "Why do you say that?" This will help to formulate a clear picture of what students actually believe about various topics. Here are some topics you can explore with your children:

- Is college important?
- What does success look like to you? *(this is fun vision board activity!)*
- Does racism still exist today?
- If someone is talking about you behind your back, what should you do?

- How does a person know if he/she is experiencing depression/anxiety and what should be done?

You can use any relevant topic. Just be sure to consult your school counselor/therapist for certain sensitive topics because, as they begin unpacking some of these topics, students may need additional emotional support.

What are some ways to change dysfunctional beliefs?

There are many ways to challenge dysfunctional beliefs and help students adopt more functional and empowered belief systems. Start by having your students identify a few goals and describe why it is important to them to accomplish those goals. You can now use this information to hold them accountable; showing them how each of their actions is bringing them closer to their goals or taking them further away. Instead of being an adversary telling them what they are doing is right or wrong, you become an ally helping to move them closer to accomplishing their goals.

Anther idea is to invite guest speakers to share their personal stories on teen pregnancy, STDs, mental illness, incarceration, and any other topic relevant to your students' needs. Allowing students to ask questions to someone with first-hand experience will benefit your students in ways a textbook never could.

What are some functional beliefs that could lead to more productive behavior?

The last step is to help students adopt more functional and empowered beliefs. Some of the beliefs students hold will literally hold them back from seeing the success they want in their lives. Here are some examples of some dysfunctional beliefs that I have addressed with my students:

Dysfunctional Belief	Functional Belief
"College is a waste of money"	College is a tool to acquire skills and knowledge that may give you a better advantage in today's competitive work force. If used wisely it can be worth the investment!
If I don't have sex with my boyfriend, he will leave me.	I am valuable and worth the wait. If he can't respect my wishes, then he should leave.

As I stated before, when it comes to SEL or any other development process, the sustainability of those results will rest in adjusting what a person believes. Practice with the call to action on the next page and put these strategies to use in your everyday life you will notice the difference.

Practice

From the list below, select an outcome you are seeing in your school or community that you would like to see changed. On the next page, complete each section of the outcome progression model using your selected outcome. On the table beneath the OPM diagram, fill in three dysfunctional belief systems that could lead to your selected outcome. Next to each dysfunctional belief, write a functional belief that would that would support a more desired outcome.

Select one of the outcomes below or create one of your own. During this process be sensitive to cultural preferences and individuality.

- Bullying
- Fighting
- Teen Pregnancy
- Truancy
- Failing
- Disrespecting authority

The Outcome Progression Model
by Hotep, Educational Success Strategist

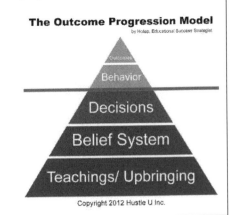

Copyright 2012 Hustle U Inc.

Outcome Progression Model

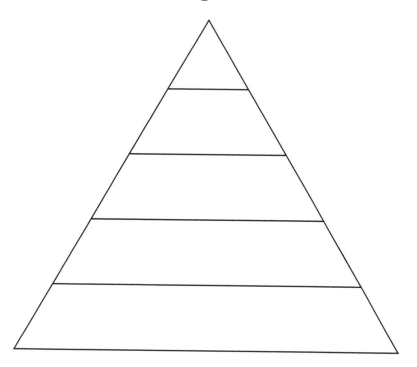

Dysfunctional Belief	Functional Belief

Bonus Secret

Emotional
Preparation

Have you noticed toward the end of summer we begin to see back-to-school displays in the entry ways of our neighborhood stores, with school shopping lists? This is their way of reminding us to make sure our students are prepared with everything they need for academic success. What items are on your "must-have" back-to-school shopping list? Fold a sheet of paper in half and on the left side of the paper write down as many items as you can think of to prepare your students for academic success.

As a person who loves to be prepared, enjoys planning, and preparing for worst case scenarios, I'm pretty sure you effortlessly listed several items to ensure your students were set up for success academically. Now, on the right side, I want you to create a list for must-have items needed for your students to succeed emotionally and socially. How did your lists compare? Did you find one to be easier than the other? Was the length of both list comparable in size? In many cases, the second list requires a little more effort. In the image below you will see just a few items I put on my must-have list.

No matter where I am in the country, I ask educators to create a SEL list for their students because if our students are not prepared to perform socially and emotionally, it will have a direct impact on academic performance. Equipping our students with SEL tools for success will help shift what we do from teaching to transforming the lives of our students.

Join A Woman's Standard and several other educators and change makers spread the importance of social-emotional learning throughout the country so we can ensure our students EQ Kits are prepared for any experience that may arise.

Resilience
Coping tools
Self-Soothing techniques
Communication
Mental and physical Safe Spaces
Critical Thinking and Reasoning
Problem Solving
Self-Established Goal and why

CREATE

Using the items you listed for emotional preparation, create a plan for equipping your students with these tools. You may have a weekly EQ preparation activity. Print them, share them with your students while educating them on how to use these tools toward their own success.

Example: "Resilience." Play "Famous Failures" video on YouTube and follow up with class discussion. Have students identify someone they admire who has demonstrated resilience and what they can learn from them.

1.

2.

3.

4.

NOTES

NOTES

NOTES

NOTES

NOTES

NOTES

NOTES

NOTES

NOTES

NOTES

REFERENCE LIST

Mehrabian, A. (2007). *Nonverbal Communication.* Transaction Publishers

Lenape Valley Foundation (2013). *Trauma Informed Care newsletter.* Lenape Valley Foundation

Hotep (2012). *The Outcome Progression Model.* Stone Mountain, GA: Hustle U. Inc.

Social Emotional Learning Resources:

Unpacking the Emotional Suitcase

Unpacking the Emotional Suitcase is a fully comprehensive activity guide designed to provide strategies to help individuals cope with emotional trauma and process the feelings that stem from those traumatic experiences. Unpacking the Emotional Suitcase can be used personally to help you achieve emotional success or professionally to facilitate the emotional development process of the population you serve.

Teach a Girl to Fish

TAGTF takes a holistic approach to youth development understanding that no sustainable learning can take place until we address the social and emotional needs of our students. The lessons shared in this book are designed to help readers overcome emotional, relational, aspirational, belief, and personal barriers. By teaching girls to think critically, problem solve, and make sound decisions we equip them to reach their full potential.

Give them the tools. Teach them the skills. Watch them thrive.

Butterfly Tales

Butterfly tales is a compilation of motivating poems and stories of trials, tribulation and triumph for girls and the ones that care for them. Butterfly tales uses the life cycle of the butterfly as an analogy to illustrate real life issues our young women are faced with on a daily basis as they transition from childhood to womanhood. Each reader will witness the journey of the slow, insecure, shy caterpillar fumbling through challenges and trying to find herself. While in her cocoon stage she becomes aware of 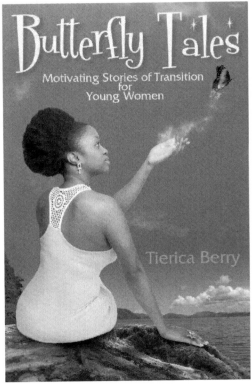 herself and sheds her insecurities and low self-esteem to find her voice. Finally she gains her confidence as she completes her last stage of metamorphosis transitioning into the strong, confident, intelligent, and beautiful butterfly she was destined to be.

Think it Over

Social Emotional Learning Activity Card Game

Think It Over is a competitive card game that infuses Social and Emotional Learning with healthy debate to deepen student engagement. Great for small groups or team mode for **peer collaboration**. All lessons are **aligned to SEL competencies** and defined in the T.I.O student handbook. At AWS, we believe student outcomes improve when we teach them how to...

Think It Over!

Girls' SEL Activity Guide

About the author

Tierica Berry is an Award-Winning author, Trainer and Social-Emotional Learning Specialist whose work has transformed the lives of thousands of teachers, leaders and students. Her deeply transformative professional development seminars guide educators and leaders in emotional intelligence, reconnecting with the disconnected and engaging the disengaged. Her expertise in the arena of social emotional learning goes hand-in-hand with culturally relevant and responsive teaching and is the key to releasing and unleashing the true potential of students.

Ms. Berry is the creator of "A Woman's Standard," a gender-based youth leadership development program designed to remove barriers for female student achievement. With heavy emphasis on literacy, emotional intelligence, and self-efficacy, Tierica has managed to motivate and redirect some of the most troubled youth with her engaging and relevant programs. Her Past clientele includes various types of youth organizations from public school districts, girls' programs, charter schools and youth detention centers.

Ms. Berry has received national recognition for her creative writing program, *The Anthology Project*, and her highly relevant program that help with transition, refinement, self-esteem, and critical thinking. She has authored multiple books for teen girls including *Unpacking the Emotional Suitcase* an activity guide for emotional success and *Teach a Girl to Fish: Lessons of Responsibility and Accountability for Young Women*. Her passion for empowering girls can be summed up in one statement, "If you want to uplift a community start with its women because it is through women that all communities are born."

To learn more about our relevant programs and impactful initiatives please visit:
www.AWomansStandard.com

For booking please email your request to:
Tierica@AWomansStandard.com

Made in the USA
Columbia, SC
10 December 2022

72509207R00054